SCHOLASTIC **discover more**™

My Body

By Andrea Pinnington
and Penny Lamprell

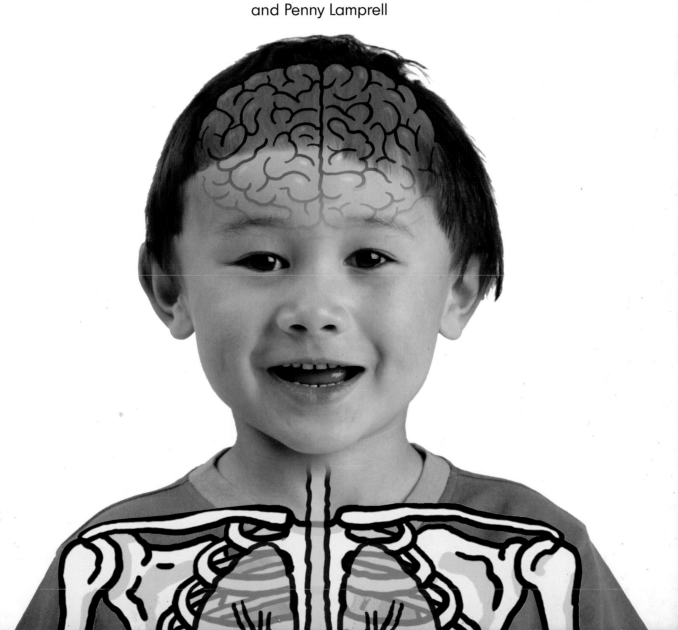

How to discover more

My Body is specially planned to help you discover more about your incredible body.

Big words and pictures introduce an important subject.

Small words help you explore pictures for active reading.

Picture sequences show what happens in detail.

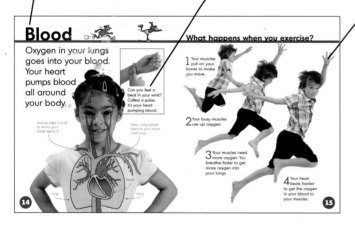

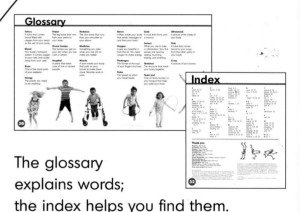

The glossary explains words; the index helps you find them.

Digital companion book

Download your free all-new digital book, **My Body Fun!**

Log on to
www.scholastic.com/ discovermore

Enter your unique code:
RMRMHP4WDDX6

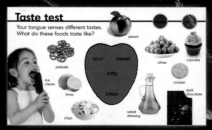

Fun body activities

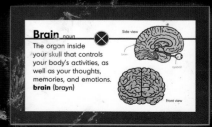

More body words

Contents

Literacy Consultant: Barbara Russ, 21st Century Community Learning Center Director for Winooski (Vermont) School District

Human Anatomy Consultant: Richard Walker, BSc, PhD

Library of Congress Cataloging-in-Publication Data Available

ISBN 978-0-545-34514-9

10 9 8 7 6 5 4 3 2 1   12 13 14 15 16

Printed in Singapore   46
First edition, March 2012

Outside

Your body is amazing. Can you name all its parts?

hand

head

eye

arm

ear

nose

mouth

finger

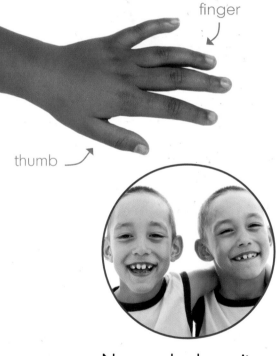

thumb

knee

leg

No one looks quite like you, unless you are an identical twin.

foot

toe

Inside

Here are the parts you would see if you looked under your skin.

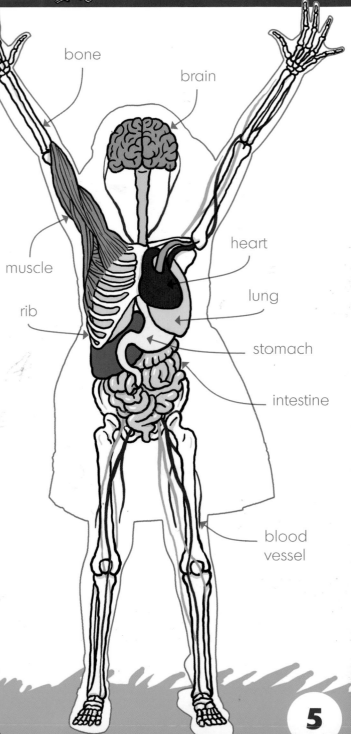

bone

brain

muscle

rib

heart

lung

stomach

intestine

blood vessel

Point to your:

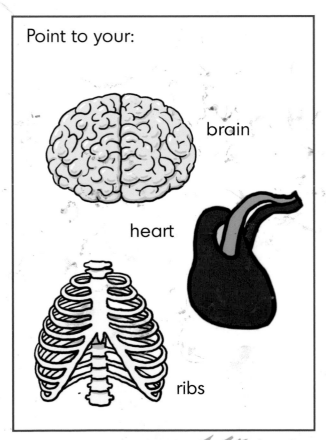

brain

heart

ribs

Hair

Hair grows on almost every part of your body. It protects you and keeps you warm.

What color is your hair?

Your hair isn't alive. That's why it doesn't hurt when it is cut.

The hair on your head grows about 6 inches (15 cm) a year.

Skin

Your skin protects your insides and keeps your body at the right temperature.

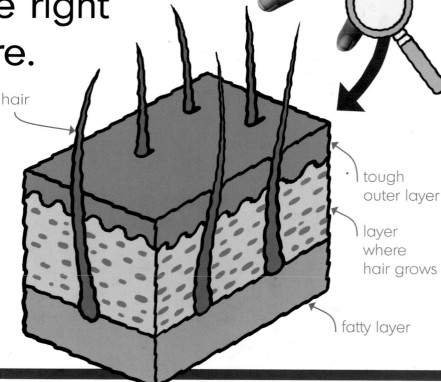

hair

tough outer layer

layer where hair grows

fatty layer

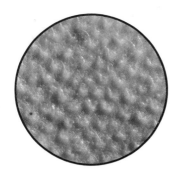

Goose bumps raise the hairs on your skin, trapping heat to warm you up.

Your skin gets more wrinkly as you get older.

18-month-old

14-year-old

60-year-old

7

Bones

Your bones keep your body parts together and help you move. They help protect your insides, too.

All your bones together are called your skeleton.

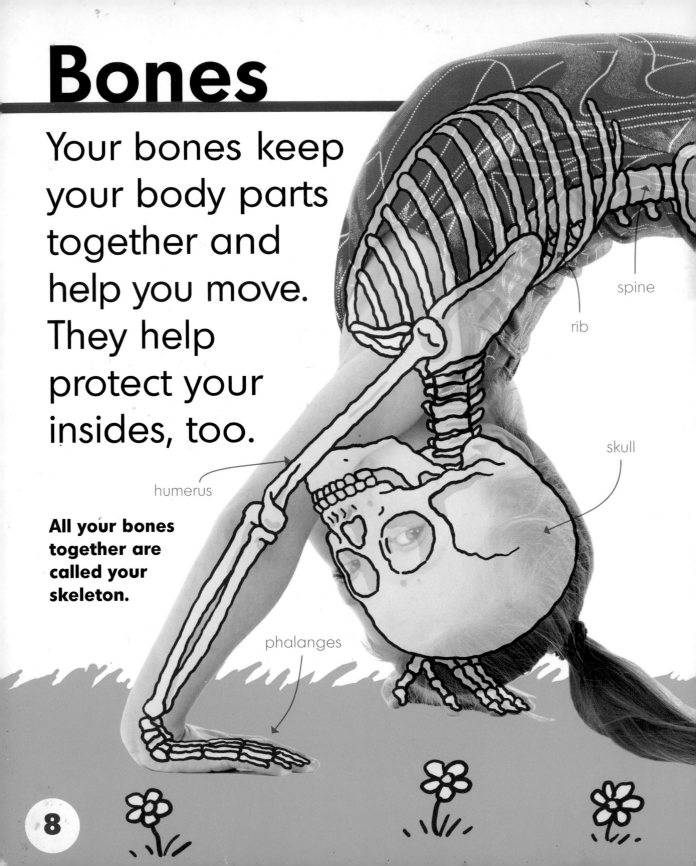

spine

rib

skull

humerus

phalanges

8

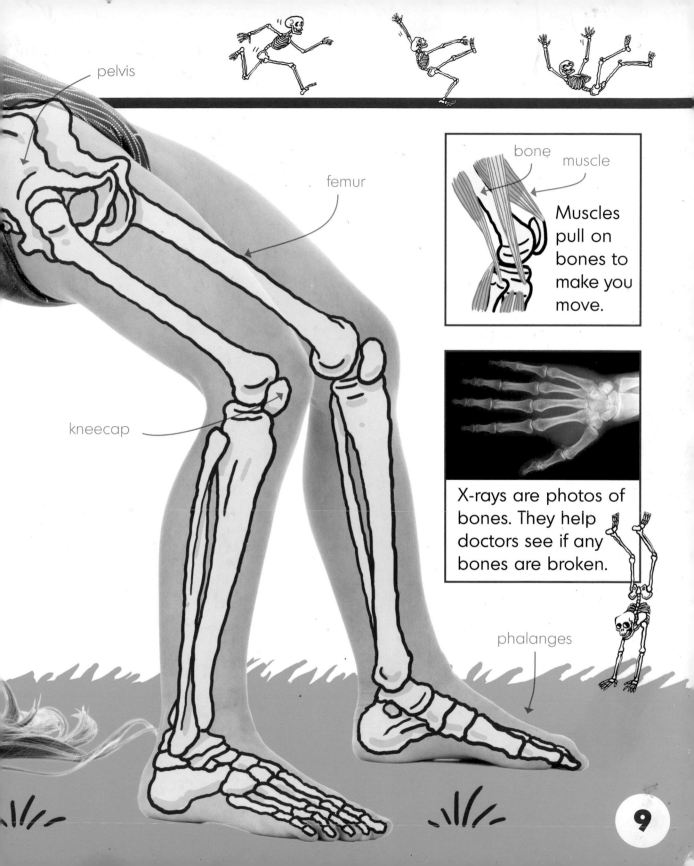

pelvis

femur

kneecap

phalanges

bone

muscle

Muscles pull on bones to make you move.

X-rays are photos of bones. They help doctors see if any bones are broken.

Who's in charge?

Your brain controls what you think, feel, and do. It sends and receives messages to and from your body.

Your brain is busy even when you are sleeping.

It controls actions you don't think about, like breathing.

Your brain controls your thoughts and movements.

It makes memories, like of places you have lived.

brain

Train your brain

Look at these things for a minute, then close the book. What can your brain remember?

wizard's hat

lemon

jump rope

skeleton

spider

penguin

balloon

cupcake

glasses

flower

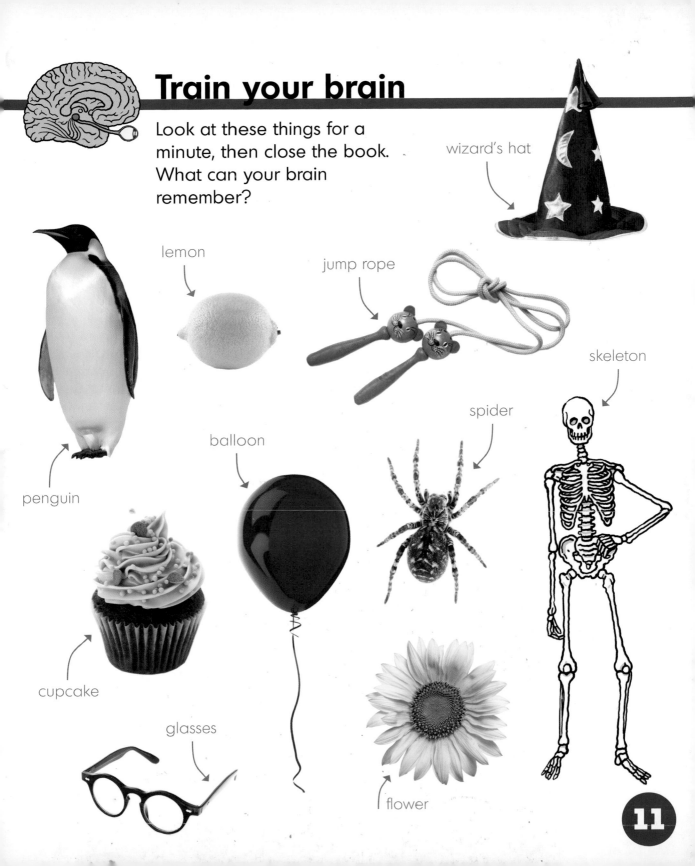

Breathing

You breathe air to get the oxygen your body needs.

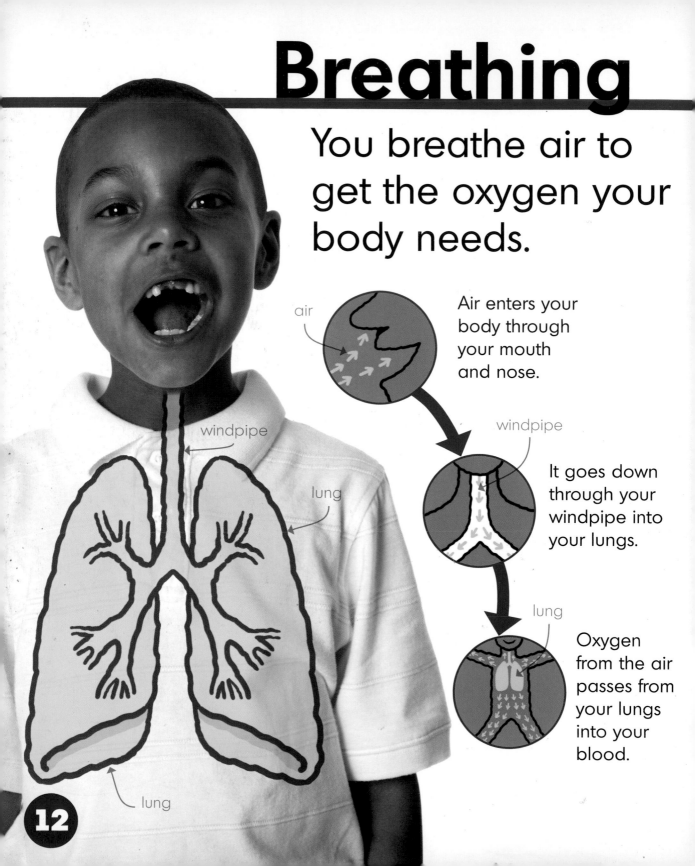

windpipe

lung

lung

air

Air enters your body through your mouth and nose.

windpipe

It goes down through your windpipe into your lungs.

lung

Oxygen from the air passes from your lungs into your blood.

You breathe about 18,000 times a day!

Try breathing onto a mirror. It mists up because your breath is warm and wet.

Breathing out gets rid of waste your body doesn't need.

Blood

Oxygen in your lungs goes into your blood. Your heart pumps blood all around your body.

Can you feel a beat in your wrist? Called a pulse, it's your heart pumping blood.

Arteries take blood to where your body needs it.

Veins carry blood back to your heart and lungs.

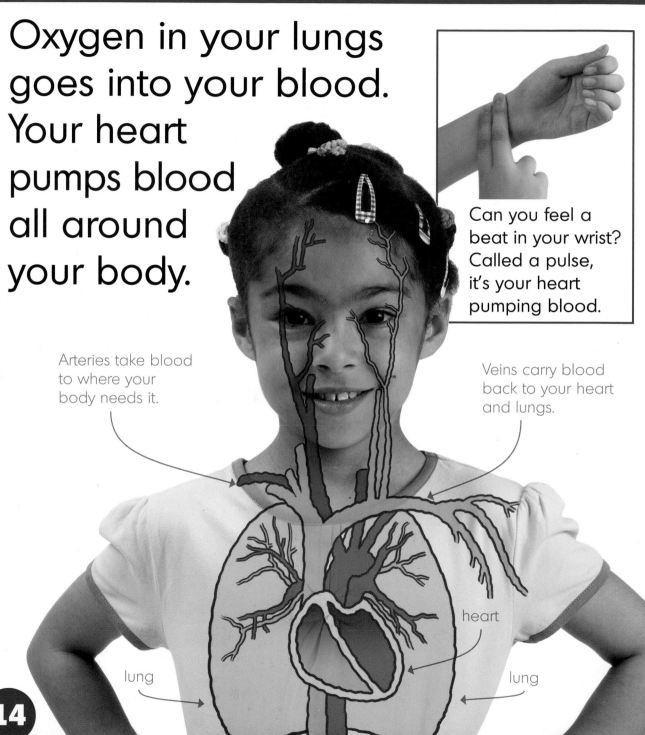

heart

lung

lung

14

What happens when you exercise?

1 Your muscles pull on your bones to make you move.

2 Your busy muscles use up oxygen.

3 Your muscles need more oxygen. You breathe faster to get more oxygen into your lungs.

4 Your heart beats harder to get the oxygen in your blood to your muscles.

Senses

Your senses help make you
aware of the world around you.

Hearing
What can you
hear right now?

Seeing
What do you
see right now?

Touching
What do these
gloves feel like?

Tasting
What's your
favorite taste?

Smelling
What's the worst
smell you can
think of?

Hearing

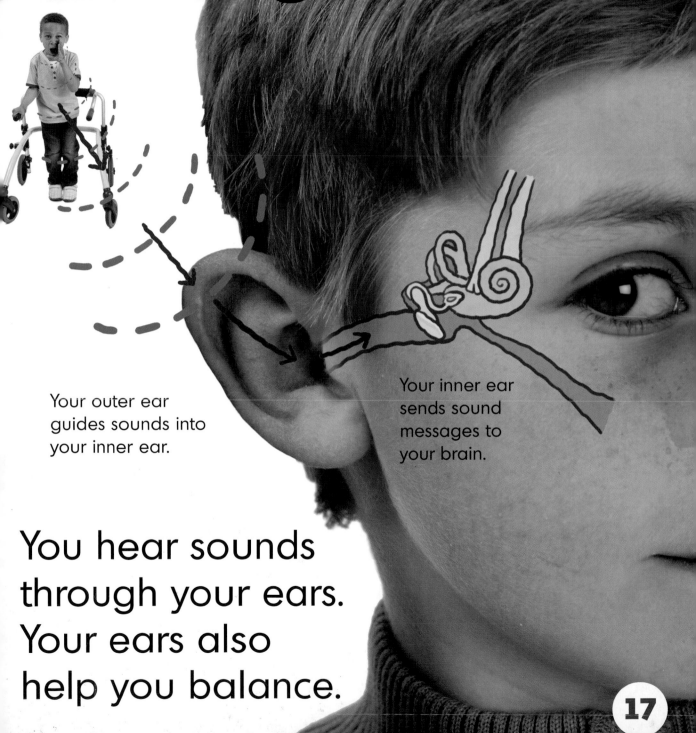

Your outer ear guides sounds into your inner ear.

Your inner ear sends sound messages to your brain.

You hear sounds through your ears. Your ears also help you balance.

Seeing

Your eyes send messages to your brain about what you see.

Glasses help people see better.

Light enters your eye. It then makes a picture of what you see.

Your eye sends this picture message to your brain.

What can you see?

Sometimes your brain can't figure out what you are seeing. Do you see a rabbit or a duck here?

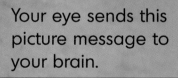

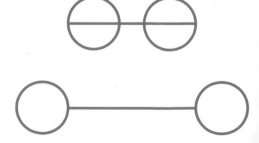

Look at the straight lines. Which line is longer?

Touching

You touch things with your skin to find out how they feel.

People who cannot see read by touching raised dots called Braille.

Nerve endings under your skin tell your brain about the things you touch.

How do these things feel?

Hard or soft?

Prickly or smooth?

Tasting

You have lots of tiny bumps on your tongue. These tell you what your food tastes like.

Look at your tongue in the mirror. Can you see the bumps?

The tiny bumps on your tongue are called taste buds.

sour

sweet

salty

bitter

These are some of the tastes your tongue can sense.

Smelling

You smell with your nose. Smelling food helps your sense of taste.

Smells travel through the air and up your nose.

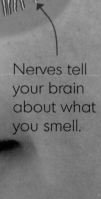

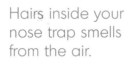

Hairs inside your nose trap smells from the air.

Nerves tell your brain about what you smell.

It's hard to smell when your nose is stuffed up.

Eating

Food gives you energy. Energy is the power your body needs to do its jobs.

mouth →

1 You chew with your teeth to break up your food.

2 The food travels down a tube into your stomach.

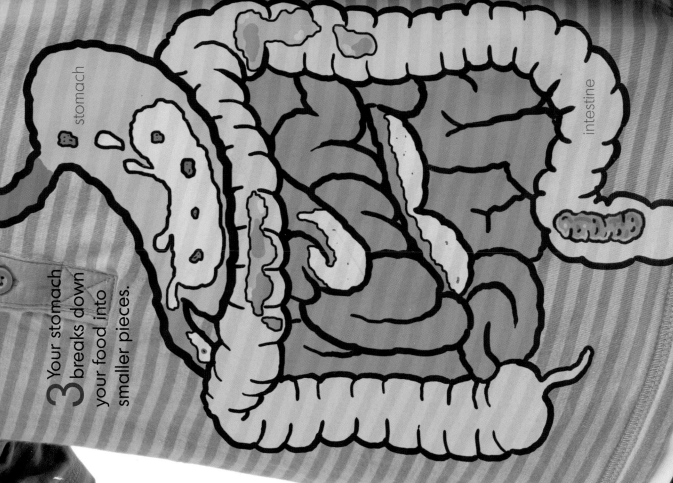

stomach

intestine

3 Your stomach breaks down your food into smaller pieces.

4 These pieces travel into a long tube called your intestine.

5 Tiny bits of food go into your blood to give you energy.

6 Food you don't need comes out as waste.

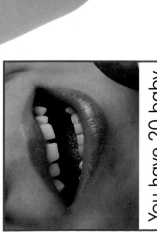

You have 20 baby teeth. As these fall out, you get 32 adult teeth.

Fit and healthy

You need to take care of your body to stay healthy. How many of these things do you do?

Do you eat healthy food?

Do you get a lot of exercise?

Do you drink enough water?

Do you get plenty of sleep?

Your body needs:

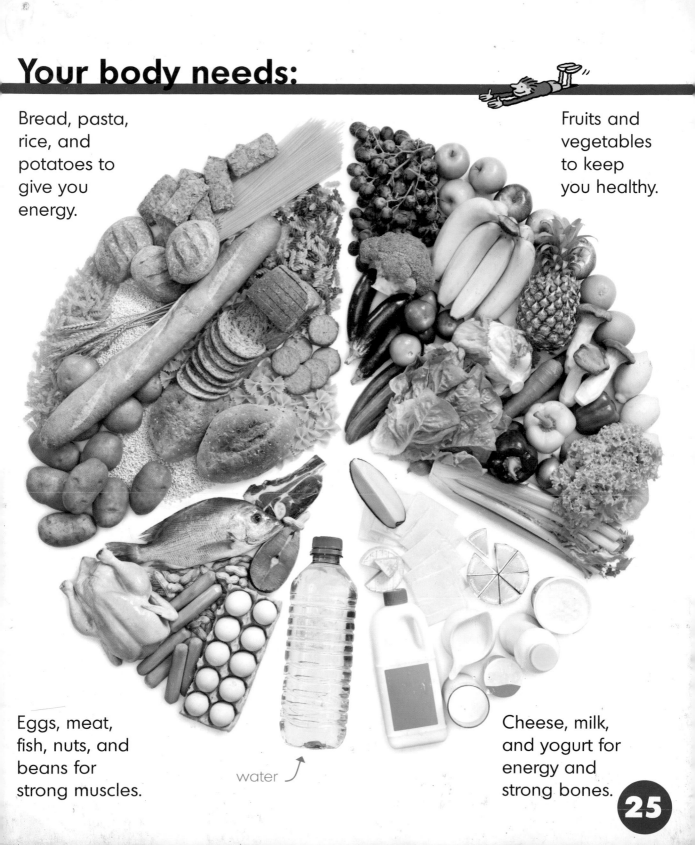

Bread, pasta, rice, and potatoes to give you energy.

Fruits and vegetables to keep you healthy.

Eggs, meat, fish, nuts, and beans for strong muscles.

water

Cheese, milk, and yogurt for energy and strong bones.

25

Starting out

A baby starts inside a woman's body. It grows and grows until it is ready to be born.

This is a special picture of a baby before it has been born. The picture is called an ultrasound.

Growing up

Your body is always changing. It will take 18 years for you to become an adult.

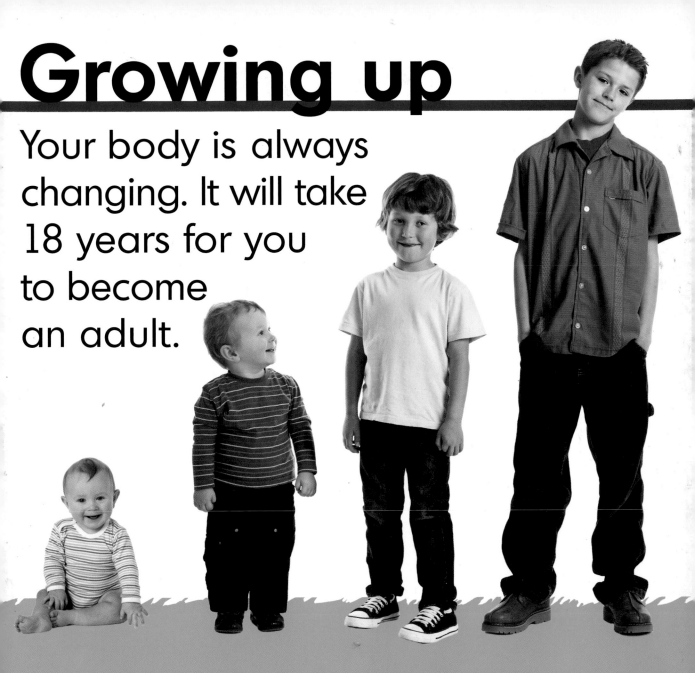

0–12 months
When you are a baby, you can't do very much at all.

1–4 years
You can walk and talk. You are learning all the time.

5–12 years
You are losing your baby teeth. You now go to school.

13–18 years
You are growing fast. You will soon be an adult.

27

Getting better

Your body knows when it's not well. It works hard to make itself better.

Bandages are useful if you hurt yourself.

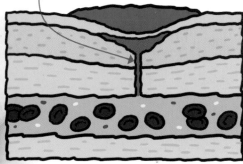

skin wound

hard scab

Your body knows if you cut yourself. Your blood helps make a scab to seal the wound.

If you don't feel well, you might be given some medicine.

It's good to see a doctor if you don't get better quickly.

Usually, you go to the hospital or a clinic if you break a bone.

Sometimes people have to stay in the hospital to get better.

29

Glossary

Artery
A tube that carries blood filled with oxygen from your heart to the rest of your body.

Blood
Your body's transport system. It carries oxygen to your cells and waste away from your cells.

Bone
One of the hard parts of your skeleton.

Energy
The power you need to do anything.

Femur
The leg bone that runs from your pelvis to your knee.

Goose bumps
The bumps you get on your skin when you are cold or afraid.

Hospital
A place that takes care of sick or injured people.

Humerus
The arm bone that runs from your shoulder to your elbow.

Medicine
Something you take when you are sick to make you better.

Muscle
A part inside your body that pulls on your bones to make them move. Muscles work in pairs.

Nerve
A fiber inside your body that sends messages to and from your brain.

Oxygen
A gas you breathe in from the air. You need oxygen to make energy.

Phalanges
The bones at the tops of your fingers and toes.

Pulse
The speed at which your heart beats.

Scab
A crust that forms over a wound.

Senses
What you use to take in information. Your five senses are hearing, seeing, touching, tasting, and smelling.

Skeleton
The structure that holds your body together.

Taste bud
One of many bumps on your tongue that help you taste your food.

Ultrasound
A picture of the inside of your body.

Vein
A tube that carries blood to your lungs from the other parts of your body.

X-ray
A picture of your bones.

Index

Thank you

Illustrator: Ellis Nadler
Art Director: Bryn Walls
Designer: Penny Lamprell
Managing Editor: Miranda Smith
US Editor: Beth Sutinis
Cover Designer: Natalie Godwin
DTP: John Goldsmid
Picture Researchers: Alan Gottlieb, Dwayne Howard
Executive Director of Photography, Scholastic: Steve Diamond
Photographer: Paul Close
Models: Adam, Charlie, Dashiel, Edith, Fidel, Grace, Jack, Jasmine, Laura, Noah, and Yasmin
Front cover model: Ruby Gawe

Photography credits
All photography by Paul Close except for the following: 4tl: Steve Shott/Getty Images; 4bl, 4r: iStockphoto; 6mr: Jose Luis Pelaez, Inc./Blend Images/Corbis; 7tr: iStockphoto; 7ml: Tyler Olsen/Shutterstock; 7bl, 7bm: iStockphoto; 7br: simpleman/Shutterstock; 8-9, 9br: iStockphoto; 11 (wizard's hat): Chamille White/Shutterstock; 11 (jump rope): ryby/Shutterstock; 11 (lemon): valzan/Shutterstock; 11 (penguin): Jan Martin Will/Shutterstock; 11 (cupcake): Ruth Black/Shutterstock; 11 (balloon): zooropa/Shutterstock; 11 (spider): Sergey Goruppa/Shutterstock; 11 (glasses): Anna Hoychuk/Shutterstock; 11 (flower): Tischenko Irina/

Shutterstock; 12, 13: iStockphoto; 18ml: LWA/Jay Newman/Media Bakery; 19ml: Alsu/Shutterstock; 19r: Voronin76/Shutterstock; 19bl: Media Bakery; 19bc: Alekcey/Shutterstock; 19br: italianestro/Shutterstock; 20 (sour): Aleksandr Bryliaev/Shutterstock; 20 (sweet): Aaron Amat/Shutterstock; 20 (salty): Roxana Bashyrova/Shutterstock; 20 (bitter): alejandro dans neergaard/Shutterstock; 21 (orange): Valentyn Volkov/Shutterstock; 25 (water): thumb/Shutterstock; 25 (food): ifong/Shutterstock; 26bl: Chad Ehlers-Stock Connection/Science Faction/Corbis; 26c: iStockphoto; 27r: Photodisc/Getty Images; 27l, 27ml, 27mr: iStockphoto; 28l: Jaimie Duplass/Shutterstock; 28r: Michael Hitoshi/Getty Images; 29t: iStockphoto; 29c: George Doyle/Getty Images.

Cover credits
Front tr: iStockphoto; c (young girl): Gary Ombler. Back tl, tc: iStockphoto; tr: Stockbyte/Getty Images.